GOD'S LAWS OF LEARNING

By
J. Paul Reno
Pastor and Author

GOD'S LAWS OF LEARNING

Copyrighted © by Pastor J. Paul Reno
Hagerstown, MD
January, 2016

ISBN 978-0-9860730-6-9

Published by
Blessed Hope Publishers
Hagerstown, Md.

Publishing and Formatting Assisted by
The Old Paths Publications
142 Gold Flume Way
Cleveland, GA 30528
Web address: www.theoldpathspublications.com
Email address: TOP@theoldpathspublications.com

All Scripture quotations in this book are taken from the King James Version of the Bible.

"All scripture is given by inspiration of God, and is profitable for doctrine, for reproof, for correction, for instruction in righteousness.

That the man of God may be perfect, throughly furnished unto all good works."

(II Tim. 3:16, 17)

DEDICATION

Dedicated to the memory of my Aunt Evelyn Reno and Miss Bernice Jordan, who prayed for and encouraged me much in my youth. Their gentle Christian manner helped me greatly.

Further, I dedicate this to the memory of Herman and Vivian Harvey who poured much into me while I was in their youth group.

Pastor J. Paul Reno

January, 2016

THIS PAGE IS FOR YOUR PERSONAL NOTES

FOREWORD

The following is a result of much Bible reading, meditation, prayer and practical application. God has blessed me and I want to share these insights. I trust that you the reader will study the scriptures and make great progress on this subject.

We have lost so much that needs to be recovered.

May God bless all of you through the Bible (KJV) to expand your learning ability towards our created potential.

Pastor J. Paul Reno
January, 2016

GOD'S LAWS OF LEARNING

THIS PAGE IS FOR YOUR PERSONAL NOTES

TABLE OF CONTENTS

DEDICATION	3
FOREWORD	5
TABLE OF CONTENTS	7
PREFACE	11
CHAPTER 1: GOD'S LAWS OF LEARNING	**13**
Proverbs 1:5a	13
II Timothy 3:14-15	14
CHAPTER 2: GOD'S PROMISES FOR LEARNING	**19**
Proverbs 3:13	19
Proverbs: 4:10	19
Proverbs 24:3	20
Proverbs 24:4	20
Proverbs 24:5	20
Proverbs 14:6	21
Proverbs 1:7a	22
Proverbs 1:29	23
Proverbs 2:1-6	23
Proverbs 9:10	25
Proverbs 16:3	25
Proverbs 28:5	26
CHAPTER 3: THE VALUE OF LEARNING	**29**
Proverbs 3:13-15	29
Proverbs 8:10, 11	29
Proverbs 16:16	30
THE VALUE OF LEARNING	**30**
CHAPTER 4: ATTITUDES FOR LEARNING	**31**
Proverbs 3:5	31
1. DON'T LOOK TO YOUR OWN ABILITIES.	31
2. LEARN TO FEAR THE LORD.	32
3. DEPART FROM EVIL.	32
Proverbs 11:2	33
Proverbs 9:2-6	33
Proverbs 16:21	33
Proverbs 8:17	34
Proverbs 12:1	35
Proverbs 13:16	35

Proverbs 13:20	36
I Corinthians 1:30	36

CHAPTER 5: FIVE RULES FOR LEARNING — 39

1. LEARN TO HEAR OR LISTEN — 39
   - Proverbs 1:5a — 39
   - Proverbs 5:7 — 39
   - Proverbs 13:1 — 39
   - Proverbs 15:32b — 40
2. PAY ATTENTION — 40
   - Proverbs 4:1 — 40
   - Proverbs 4:20 — 41
   - Proverbs 5:1 — 41
3. SEEK AFTER KNOWLEDGE — 42
   - Proverbs 8:17 — 42
   - Proverbs 8:14 — 42
   - Proverbs 15:14 — 42
   - Proverbs 17:16 — 43
   - Proverbs 18:1, 2 — 43
4. APPLY YOURSELF — 44
   - Proverbs 22:17 — 44
   - Proverbs 23:12 — 44
5. GET IT AND KEEP IT — 45
   - Proverbs 4:5 — 45
   - Proverbs 4:13 — 45
   - Proverbs 4:4 — 45

CHAPTER 6: SIX METHODS OF INSTRUCTION — 47

1. TEACHING BY PROVERBS — 47
   - Proverbs 1:1-4 — 47
2. REPROVING — 48
   - Proverbs 19:25 — 48
3. PROPER USE OF THE ROD AND REPROOF — 48
   - Proverbs 29:15a — 48
4. TEACH PEOPLE TO FEAR GOD — 49
   - Proverbs 1:7 — 49
5. HEARING WHAT'S SPOKEN — 49
   - Proverbs 2:1 — 49
6. INSTRUCTION BEING GIVEN — 50
   - Proverbs 4:1 — 50

CHAPTER 7: DANGERS OF OPPOSING LEARNING — 51

- Proverbs 1:7 — 51

TABLE OF CONTENTS

Proverbs 1:22	51
Proverbs 1:28, 29	52
Proverbs 5:12, 13	52
Proverbs 12:1	53
Proverbs 18:2	54
CHAPTER 8: THREE THINGS THAT HINDER LEARNING	**55**
1. FOOLISHNESS	55
Proverbs 9:13	55
Proverbs 15:14	55
Proverbs 17:24	55
Proverbs 18:2	56
Proverbs 22:15	56
2. WICKEDNESS	56
Proverbs 17:4	56
3. LISTENING TO WRONG TEACHING	57
Proverbs 19:27	57
CHAPTER 9: THREE PROBLEMS OF IGNORANCE	**59**
1. DESTRUCTION	59
Proverbs 10:14	59
2. DEATH	59
Proverbs 10:21	59
3. FINANCES	60
Proverbs 17:16	60
INDEX OF WORDS AND PHRASES	**61**
ABOUT THE AUTHOR	**67**

THIS PAGE IS FOR YOUR PERSONAL NOTES

PREFACE

It is amazing but true – you can improve your ability to learn! I did not learn these principles in 18+ years of education nor from a book. They were discovered through ongoing Bible reading.

I am convinced that our forefathers knew these Bible principles. It seems quite evident that our culture adopted them, particularly in the area of education. I think it is only too obvious that they have been replaced by humanistic philosophy, resulting in less real learning.

In the 1950's my father, a high school principal, teacher and guidance counselor, stated that conversion resulted in an average increase of IQ scores of approximately 10 points. That seems perfectly consistent with Bible teaching.

I have watched these laws produce increased learning from kindergarten through old age in those who will allow God to assist them.

Pastor J. Paul Reno
January, 2016

THIS PAGE IS FOR YOUR PERSONAL NOTES

CHAPTER 1

GOD'S LAWS OF LEARNING

"A wise man will hear, and will increase learning;"

Proverbs 1:5a

This book is about 'getting smart' by applying God's laws of learning. If we belong to Him, there's no limit to what we can learn. Time is the only issue.

From the moment we're born our brains become built-in tools for learning – a storage room that needs to be filled – a computer that needs to be programmed – a massive filing cabinet that needs to be organized – an engine that needs fuel.

Like most, we tend to think we're either born smart or not. The truth is, under normal circumstances the brain of slow learners, average learners, above-average learners, and geniuses all appear identical. The moment we grasp "God's laws of learning" we open doors to better understanding the Bible, as well as many other things.

Obviously, some factors can adversely influence one's ability to effectively learn. Birth and heredity might have an influence. Other concerns include breaking God's rules, poor attitudes, exposure to inappropriate conversations, alcohol and drugs, how we're raised, whether we're saved, and the sins of the fathers visited on the children.

Additionally, the very tools we choose can either handicap or enhance our learning experience. For example:

- On-line information gathered in short bursts and bytes

could handicap our ability to concentrate for long periods.
- Television gives us all the sights, sounds, and words, thereby, actually keeping us from thinking.
- Radio gives us the sounds and words. We are then left to imagine the sights.
- Reading gives us only the words. We have to think and imagine the sounds and sights.

By far, reading remains the preferred method of learning. This is because it makes us think more.

Now, based on the Word of God, and what it teaches, we can begin to lay the foundation for future learning….

> *"But continue thou in the things which thou hast learned and hast been assured of, knowing of whom thou hast learned them: And that from a child thou hast known the holy scriptures, which are able to make thee wise unto salvation through faith which is in Christ Jesus."*
>
> **II Timothy 3:14-15**

Sometimes we underestimate just how much a child can learn from the Bible. Instead, we let them occupy their minds in places other than the Word of God. The phrase "from a child" means to start as a child to know the Scriptures and then continue into teenager and adulthood years. An avid reader of God's Word, Timothy was a young man before he heard about Jesus, yet he knew the Old Testament Scriptures "that could make him wise unto salvation."

In his childhood years, Timothy learned without the tools and conveniences available today. He didn't have Bible story books, Sunday school classes, Missionary Helper's Club, or a

CHAPTER 1: GOD'S LAWS OF LEARNING

whole lot of other things. His father wasn't a Christian; he was a Greek worshipper of pagan gods. Because of this, Timothy didn't have a father and grandfather to teach him. Instead, it was his godly mother Eunice and grandmother Lois.

In **John chapter 2**, we see fishermen and a tax collector. They were an odd group of men, who worked in various jobs. They weren't among those that had been trained in the University or in the Seminary at Jerusalem. They came from Galilee, a hillbilly area with an accent of its own. They knew where Peter was from because of how he spoke.

Jesus had been cleansing the temple in Jerusalem in **John 2:17**, *"And his disciples remembered that it was written, The zeal of thine house hath eaten me up."*

The disciples remembered a 'phrase' of the Scriptures and understood its application. They may never have owned a personal copy of the Bible, and yet they remembered what they had heard and read in the synagogue. It stuck in their minds. Most likely, the synagogue was thrilled to have a complete set of Old Testament Scriptures from which to study. Copies were handwritten and few and far between.

In **Luke chapter 2**, the Bible tells us, *"Jesus grew in wisdom and in stature."* When they delivered the scrolls in the synagogue at Nazareth, Jesus opened the book of Isaiah and began to read. Remember, the Bible didn't have chapter and verse divisions, punctuation in the Old Testament, vowels, or large and small letters. From the beginning of Isaiah to the end of all 66 chapters was one string of consonants. Reading from right to left, Jesus could roll through them, find what He wanted, and begin reading. How many of us know our Bibles well enough to find what we're looking for without chapters and verses?

GOD'S LAWS OF LEARNING

We're being told that people are learning more than they've ever learned before, but I doubt that. More and more, we're depending on references, reference books, and reference sources. When the Babylonians raided Israel – they not only plundered the gold and silver vessels out of the temple – they were able to abduct smiths, skilled people, and children. These Jewish children stood out as particular spoils of war. I wonder how many countries would like to raid the U.S. today to get our children because of their learning ability, especially when considering how we compare to other nations. The Babylonians wanted these children because they were vitally important to the future of the Empire.

Notice what they were looking for in **Daniel 1:4**, *"Children in whom was no blemish, but well favored, and skillful in all wisdom, and cunning in knowledge, and understanding science, and such as had ability in them to stand in the king's palace, and whom they might teach the learning and the tongue of the Chaldeans."*

In those days, there were massive libraries running into the tens and perhaps hundreds of thousands of volumes. They were looking for children that were skilled in science, had wisdom, and could learn the language. All the Chaldeans knew that with this kind of learning, these children would be a tremendous resource to their country. God had gifted His people with laws that would teach them how to learn while making them valuable in the eyes of other nations.

Is it any wonder that Joseph, who watched sheep, could oversee Potiphar's household; then turn around and run Egypt in the most difficult of times? He was a slave that had been in prison, but Joseph was also Hebrew. When Pharaoh wondered who he could get to handle this problem, realizing it had to be someone like Joseph, he turned it over to him. Neither prime

CHAPTER 1: GOD'S LAWS OF LEARNING

minister, nor any of the senators, politicians and scholars, could match Joseph. He was the one able to handle the situation – to face tragedy – and turn it into prosperity. Where did Joseph get his political training? By watching sheep and being taught at home.

How about Jacob and his ability to understand science? He could control the coloring of animals, not only at birth but also at the time of conception, thereby controlling and separating the healthy from unhealthy animals. When Laban switched things, Jacob simply changed his process and maintained control. Where had Jacob developed this skill? Not only had he been watching sheep, goats and cows, but he also had the ability to learn things that biologists still don't understand.

How about Cain – the second generation of humanity? He envisioned, planned, and built an entire city before there were people to populate it.

Without a doubt, there's so much potential in our human brains. If only we would learn to put them to work in the right way! Unfortunately, we've been so downgraded that we've convinced ourselves to believe we can't learn anything.

Listen, God's "laws of learning" could literally explode our mental capability if we would just grasp them. The evidence in the Scriptures is very clear.

THIS PAGE IS FOR YOUR PERSONAL NOTES

CHAPTER 2

GOD'S PROMISES FOR LEARNING

Now that we've seen some of the possibilities and products of learning, let's look in the book of Proverbs to see what God "promises" are the results of right and proper learning.

> *"Happy is the man that findeth wisdom, and the man that getteth understanding."*
>
> **Proverbs 3:13**

Happiness can be produced by studying and learning. People may ask, "Why do I need to know anything more? Why should I bother with learning?" Because God promises happiness to those that will seek, find wisdom, and get understanding. That makes it something to seek after.

> *"Hear, O my son, and receive my sayings: and the years of thy life shall be many."*
>
> **Proverbs: 4:10**

You can literally add to your lifespan by studying properly or shorten it by not. When I taught school, a number of students died before they graduated. Almost without exception, they were rebels in the classroom with no real interest in learning. Conversely, interested students were able to progress through school and move on. There's longevity involved. How many people have destroyed their health and future possibilities because they didn't take the time to learn how to eat right, care for their body, deal with diseases, protect themselves, and so forth? They weren't interested.

> *"Through wisdom is an house builded; and by understanding it is established."*
>
> **Proverbs 24:3**

This verse refers to more than just the physical structure of the building we live in. It takes wisdom to raise a family right. It takes wisdom and understanding to run a home right. How many homes fall apart because people won't study to learn how to raise children, how to treat their wife or husband? In sheer ignorance, the home falls apart. It takes wisdom and understanding to build it right – for it to have lasting results – for it to be established where the raising of children has long lasting results.

> *"And by knowledge shall the chambers be filled with all precious and pleasant riches."*
>
> **Proverbs 24:4**

Do you want a house that doesn't look like a yard sale special (I'm not against yard sales)? Then use wisdom and you can do very well. If you want something that's pleasing to the eye, has value, is precious, and can develop some riches, it will take knowledge. It doesn't just happen. It takes planning and studying.

> *"A wise man is strong; yea, a man of knowledge increaseth strength."*
>
> **Proverbs 24:5**

Another result of learning is its unique ability to produce strength, to teach us how to deal with people, and to care for issues. More than just physical strength, it also takes strength of the will, mind, and character. And it encompasses wisdom and knowledge. *"A man of knowledge increaseth strength."* Never satisfied, a man of knowledge always wants more. He never

CHAPTER 2: GOD'S PROMISES FOR LEARNING

knows when the next test of strength will come – and how much he's going to need.

> *"A scorner seeketh wisdom, and findeth it not; but knowledge is easy unto him that understandeth."*
>
> **Proverbs 14:6**

There comes a time when it gets easier to learn. *"Knowledge is easy unto him that understandeth."*

Pity the poor person who learns the facts, but never bothers to understand them. Sooner or later, they'll have great difficulty in even achieving a passing grade. With this in mind…

- Where is the starting point for learning?

- How does a parent get a child started right?

Much of modern education collapses because of a wrong foundation. When you start wrong, you can destroy the result or handicap the progress. Like the math teacher who decided to teach division before multiplication. It's the wrong place to start. It's always best to teach addition, then subtraction, then multiplication, and finally division. There's a proper order to it. Just try to work division problems without being able to add, subtract, and multiply. It's extremely difficult.

The same principle applies when a person begins to learn in the wrong place. It's possible. It's also very foolish. This brings us to two critical questions…

- Where should we begin on the matter of learning?

- What does God have to say in His laws on learning?

GOD'S LAWS OF LEARNING

"The fear of the LORD is the beginning of knowledge."

Proverbs 1:7a

The *"fear of the LORD"* will give you much insight on how to approach learning. The God of the Universe who created everything – including all knowledge has spoken. If you don't begin with the fear of the LORD, then you've started in the wrong place.

- Do you want to understand languages?

You need the "fear of the LORD."

- Do you want to learn mathematics?

Who set-up everything so that math would fit perfectly in a symmetrical structure? It was God.

- Do you want to study history?

It's the study of God at work – His story.

- Do you want to study science?

It's how God operates His Universe.

"The fear of the LORD is the beginning of knowledge." Leave it out, and you'll be handicapped.

At the end of verse 7, the Bible says, *"Fools despise wisdom and instruction."*

Sometimes you'll hear a person say, "I'm a fool – look at me – I'm a fool." What they're really saying is, "I don't have to learn – it's dumb – I don't need it." The Bible says to call no man a fool.

CHAPTER 2: GOD'S PROMISES FOR LEARNING

In fact, they've declared it themselves.

> *"For that they hated knowledge, and didn't choose the fear of the LORD:"*
>
> **Proverbs 1:29**

Clearly, the *"fear of the LORD"* is the result of choice. It's not something you're born with. It isn't forced upon you. You either choose it, or you don't. According to the context of this passage, if you won't fear God, then you can't expect to get started on knowledge properly. *"The fear of the LORD is the beginning of knowledge."*

> *"My son, if thou wilt receive my words, and hide my commandments with thee; So that thou incline thine ear unto wisdom, and apply thine heart to understanding; Yea, if thou criest after knowledge, and liftest up thy voice for understanding; If thou seekest her as silver, and searchest for her as for hid treasures: Then shalt thou understand the fear of the LORD, and find the knowledge of God. For the LORD giveth wisdom: out of his mouth cometh knowledge and understanding."*
>
> **Proverbs 2:1-6**

My dad used to say, "Son, you're going to have to apply yourself." That's Biblical. In other words, seeking after *"understanding and knowledge"* is more important than seeking after money. The Bible says, *"If thou seekest her as silver and searchest for her as for hid treasures..."*

Clearly, the *"fear of the LORD"* is to be understood. We ought to understand it. We ought to apply it. We ought to see where it fits into our lives. It goes along with the knowledge of God. *"The fear of the LORD is the beginning of knowledge."* And the *"knowledge of God"* is necessary if we're to get the understanding that we need.

God gives wisdom (verse 6). There are two ways to learn. You can either:

1. Drive yourself – work hard – and see if you can hang onto it.
2. Accept it – as a gift – through God's appointed means.

When I need some wisdom, understanding and knowledge – rather than trying to grasp it on my own with limited abilities – I would prefer God give it to me.

A child of God has access to learning that children of the world know little about. They pull their hair and struggle. We bow low and worship with the fear and knowledge of God. As we do, we apply ourselves. People might say, "You're a genius" when it's God's gift to those that will seek after wisdom, understanding and knowledge. That's what His Word says.

When my dad tested students in the public school system, he noticed something very interesting. The students' intelligence quotient (IQ) jumped shortly after they were saved. I'm saying, "God helps with learning." It's what He gives us when we're saved. You get a sound mind. I have personally seen unconverted students get under the Word of God, begin to fear Him, rather than to live loosely, and their grades picked-up. They improved their learning. Exposure to the Word of God, coupled with the *"fear of the LORD"* helped them achieve significant progress.

Remember, verse 1, says *"My son, if thou wilt receive my words..."* There has to be openness if we're to receive or accept what God Himself has said.

CHAPTER 2: GOD'S PROMISES FOR LEARNING

"The fear of the LORD is the beginning of wisdom: and the knowledge of the holy is understanding."

Proverbs 9:10

Not only is the *"fear of the LORD the beginning of knowledge"* but also the *"beginning of wisdom."*

The more you can understand what it means to be holy – for God to be holy – for Him to dwell in the holy realm – the more understanding you'll have regarding a multitude of things.

You'll understand why nations rise and fall. You'll understand why languages become clear and muddled. You'll understand what it takes to make things understood and confused. You'll understand the importance of math being laid out in a proper fashion. The *"fear of the LORD"* and the *"knowledge of the holy"* is necessary in the learning process.

"Commit thy works unto the LORD, and thy thoughts shall be established."

Proverbs 16:3

This verse goes along with the *"fear of the LORD,"* and the *"knowledge of the holy.."* They fit together. Do you have trouble keeping your mind on things? Do you have difficulty keeping your thoughts focused? Are they running all over the place and never settling into anything?

"Commit your works unto the LORD and your thoughts will be established." You can get them established. Listen, as long as we're trying to handle our works, instead of committing them to the LORD, our thought processes aren't going to be clear, established, or solid, and we're going to be handicapped.

GOD'S LAWS OF LEARNING

Today, more and more people are being labeled as learning disabled, while fewer are following the Word of God or have a *"fear of the LORD."* One would wonder if there is a connection between the two. People try to control their works instead of committing them to the LORD. Is it any wonder that Daniel could think clearly or Shadrach, Meshach, and Abednego? How about Joseph, Jacob, Timothy or the disciples? They followed old-fashioned Bible teaching and were able to learn.

"Evil men understand not judgment: but they that seek the LORD understand all things."

Proverbs 28:5

Those t*hat "seek the LORD"* will understand all things, not just judgment. This is what the Bible says. When you seek God, you're not hindering your learning process. A student's devotional life doesn't hinder their academic program or slow down their studies. It helps them. The time they spend *"seeking the LORD"* makes it much easier to understand.

If *you "seek the LORD"*, He will help you understand those things that seem out of your field. My mother and English teacher agreed I would never be able to write. They said, "Well, mathematics–maybe; science–maybe; history– possibly; languages and English–most definitely not…" After studying God's Word, I learned not to be discouraged. When you *"seek the LORD"*, He opens things up, and they become clear. You make distinctions, draw conclusions, and handle things that humanly are impossible. You begin to understand all things.

Don't be discouraged – *"Seek the LORD"*…You can increase your learning to the glory of God.

CHAPTER 2: GOD'S PROMISES FOR LEARNING

THIS PAGE IS FOR YOUR PERSONAL NOTES

GOD'S LAWS OF LEARNING

THIS PAGE IS FOR YOUR PERSONAL NOTES

CHAPTER 3

THE VALUE OF LEARNING

> "Happy is the man that findeth wisdom, and the man that getteth understanding. For the merchandise of it is better than the merchandise of silver, and the gain thereof than fine gold. She is more precious than rubies: and all the things thou canst desire are not to be compared unto her."
>
> Proverbs 3:13-15

A person must value learning the same way that God does, like wealth. They must put a high premium and value on it, along with the same diligence they would for a silver mine or hidden treasure.

In other words, wisdom and understanding are worth far more than any form or quantity of material wealth. The benefits of learning are far superior to anything the greatest wealth can ever produce.

> "Receive my instruction, and not silver; and knowledge rather than choice gold. For wisdom is better than rubies; and all the things that may be desired are not to be compared to it."
>
> Proverbs 8:10, 11

Silver, gold, rubies and all other things of great wealth, don't even compare to what a person gets when they set themselves to studying.

We live in such a materialistic society that people will choose money over learning. That's disobedience to the Word of God. The knowledge to be gained is far above choice gold, better than silver, and more precious than rubies.

It's important to obtain an education before getting a job – to keep one's priorities straight – to avoid the heartbreak of making wrong choices. It becomes so much easier when you put God's value on learning first. That's what the Bible teaches.

> "How much better is it to get wisdom than gold!
> and to get understanding rather than to be chosen
> than silver!

Proverbs 16:16

A proper education is far better than wealth. We're to value learning the same way that God does. True education will cost in effort, desire, priority, and money. Instead of just passing tests and surviving courses, we need to seek to learn, know, understand, and apply knowledge to our lives.

THE VALUE OF LEARNING

If it doesn't cost – it won't be valued

&

What's not valued– is soon forgotten

CHAPTER 4

ATTITUDES FOR LEARNING

In addition to a high value, learning requires a proper attitude.

> *"Trust in the LORD with all thine heart; and lean not unto thine own understanding."*
>
> **Proverbs 3:5**

When it comes to one's attitude, there's a definite need to trust God for the ability to learn. How often do we trust in our own abilities only to feel disabled? God has promised to give us the ability we need.

To be able to learn: *"Trust in the LORD with all thine heart."*

To understand all things: *"Seek the LORD."*

> *"Be not wise in thine own eyes; fear the LORD, and depart from evil."*
>
> **Proverbs 3:7**

There are three principles in this verse...

1. DON'T LOOK TO YOUR OWN ABILITIES.

People who trust in their own abilities or think they're smart, generally hit a brick wall, bounce off, and say, "That's not supposed to happen. It's always been easy for me. I ought to float by this." God is humbling them.

In the past, saints of God from the most common of families could read their Bibles at the age of four. This included the Old

Testament in Hebrew, as well as the New Testament in Greek. There were English speaking youngsters who went to college at the age of 10 or 11, and graduated as young as 14 or 15 years of age.

The oldest center of higher learning in the U.S., Harvard University, was founded in 1636. During that time, the final exam included a passage from the Old Testament in Hebrew and the New Testament in Greek, which was then translated into English. Students also translated the Greek into Hebrew, the Hebrew into Greek, and both into French, Spanish, Italian, and German. They interpreted passages with appropriate comments that were considered satisfactory theologically in each of those languages. Their grammar and spelling was expected to be correct. Today, I know of no university in the world that has such a test for a bachelor's degree. How did they do it? They learned to *"seek the LORD"* instead of looking to themselves.

2.   LEARN TO FEAR THE LORD.

In addition to seeking the LORD, you must learn to fear Him. After all, the *"fear of the LORD is the beginning of knowledge."* That's where it starts. Learn to fear God.

3.   DEPART FROM EVIL.

Not only do you need to *"fear the LORD"*, you also need to *"depart from evil."* Those who get into sin handicap their ability to learn. That's why even secular colleges and schools used to have moral standards. The teachers recognized a relationship between morality and learning, whether it was lying, stealing, cursing, adultery, or an inability to learn. Their job was always to educate; consequently, they wanted students to learn how to depart from evil. Don't stand around resisting evil. Get away from it!

Today, we see more and more learning disabilities because we don't depart from evil, and we don't *"fear the LORD."* Instead,

CHAPTER 4: ATTITUDES FOR LEARNING

we teach people to lean on their own understanding, – to be wise in their own eyes.

> *"When pride cometh, then cometh shame: but with the lowly is wisdom."*
>
> **Proverbs 11:2**

A person who's humble and lowly will attain wisdom – making progress as they plow forward. God is going to assist them. Meanwhile, sooner or later, the proud will only bring shame to the learner. It's what the Bible teaches.

> *"She hath killed her beasts; she hath mingled her wine; she hath also furnished her table. She hath sent forth her maidens: she crieth upon the highest places of the city, Whoso is simple, let him turn in hither: as for him that wanteth understanding, she saith to him, Come, eat of my bread, and drink of the wine which I have mingled. Forsake the foolish, and live; and go in the way of understanding."*
>
> **Proverbs 9:2-6**

These verses talk about "wisdom" in picture language. They represent a delightful portrait of wisdom, knowledge, and the ability to apply them in given situations. They say we ought to have the mindset that, given the opportunity to learn, it's like being invited to a banquet with the chance to feast on knowledge. Not just for knowledge's sake, but for wisdom, too. Yet instead of anticipating a beautiful banquet, we dodge the knowledge and learning. We avoid the banquet and miss the opportunity to learn.

> *"The wise in heart shall be called prudent: and the sweetness of the lips increaseth learning."*
>
> **Proverbs 16:21**

We don't have to think long and hard before we understand the importance of being *"called prudent"* and of having *"sweetness of lips."*

Consider the student who is rude to the teacher, as opposed to the one with sweetness of lips. I would venture to say, the latter increased their learning while the former did not. In other words, the *"sweetness of lips"* or *"politeness of speech"* increases one's ability to learn. Rudeness and bad manners make for learning disabilities. How many parents, by not teaching their children the proper ways of speech and manners, have handicapped them from ever learning? *"The sweetness of the lips increaseth learning."* Conversely, parents that teach their children good manners have prepared them, not only to learn, but to increase their abilities and opportunities. That is what God says.

When my dad taught in private school, he refused to answer questions that weren't graciously presented. Students that didn't shape up were disciplined. You might say, "That's harsh." Maybe so, but sometime later, a former student said the lessons helped him to learn, especially how Dad made them behave and speak in class. It left a positive mark, one that he never forgot. The man went on to serve the Lord on the mission field. My dad quit teaching at that school back in 1949. Today, that man still recalls his life changing experience.

> "I love them that love me; and those that seek me early shall find me."
>
> **Proverbs 8:17**

This verse talks about wisdom's relationship to the matter of knowledge and learning. Wisdom loves those that love it. On the other hand, those that have a bad attitude rarely learn very much. They say, "I hate this." Then it's all downhill from there. If

CHAPTER 4: ATTITUDES FOR LEARNING

parents could only get their children to love education – to love learning – it would help them greatly. *"Those that seek me early shall find me."*

Priorities need to be set early – put on the top of the list in life – instead of waiting too long until it's too late. Parents that mock or downgrade education are handicapping their children with a learning disability they weren't born with. This is serious business. It's not to be taken lightly.

"Whoso loveth instruction loveth knowledge: but he that hateth reproof is brutish."

Proverbs 12:1

This verse has a similar connotation to the one above, except it talks about loving the process by which you learn. You can learn to love instruction. You need a form of instruction that fits.

It's good to have an outline and points to illustrate. If students could learn to love the process of instruction – they would also come to love the knowledge they get by it. How often do society, television and other such things serve to destroy one's attitude towards learning? The very fact that some kids ever learn is a marvel. The good news: The Word of God can still bring them great release.

"Every prudent man dealeth with knowledge: but a fool layeth open his folly."

Proverbs 13:16

We all need to know how to properly deal with knowledge. A prudent person will not ignore, evade, or reject it. It might be hard, but they will find a way to deal with the facts. God says if we would seek Him, He will help us.

"The fear of the LORD is the beginning of knowledge."

Conversely, *"a fool layeth open his folly."*

A fool will refuse to deal with knowledge. Then he will want to know why he can't read, why he can't work certain jobs, why he can't adjust to this and that – all because of the poor choices he made. He refused to deal with knowledge and it cost him greatly.

> *"He that walketh with wise men shall be wise: but a companion of fools shall be destroyed."*
>
> **Proverbs 13:20**

Our choice of friends can greatly affect our ability to learn. This verse says we need to find some wise people and associate with them. I count it a privilege that God has allowed me to be around some of His great saints – knowledgeable people. If you had asked me who Socrates and Plato were and what was the Pythagorean factor...my response would have been "some kind of a theorem." I didn't know the connection with Socrates and Plato, nor what that had to do with the Roman Catholic Church and the present perversions of the Word of God. Today, I know about this subject because wise saints made it possible for me to understand.

Pick the wrong kind of friends and it brings destruction. By the way, there's none wiser than the LORD Jesus. If we would only learn to walk with Him, we would be wise. We would be conformed to His image. We would be like Him. *"He that walketh with wise men shall be wise..."*

> *"But of him are ye in Christ Jesus, who of God is made unto us wisdom, and righteousness, and sanctification, and redemption."*
>
> **I Corinthians 1:30**

CHAPTER 4: ATTITUDES FOR LEARNING

We talk about how Jesus redeems, purifies, sanctifies, sets us apart, and makes us holy. This same One knew no sin, but became sin for us. Yet how often do we talk about Jesus being our wisdom?

There is an aspect of Jesus that people often ignore. It has to do with our learning ability – the ability to have wisdom for life. Some people think it's spiritual to be poor and ignorant. That is still being preached in some churches, as if a lack of knowledge makes one more spiritual.

Other people like to worship at the altar of education. That's wrong. It's idolatry. These people think they can operate in the power of the mind. We are not to lean on our own understanding. We're not to see ourselves as being wise. Jesus is wisdom. He said, *"Learn of me."* He was *"made unto us wisdom, and righteousness, and sanctification, and redemption."*

If you're going to walk with the wise, walk with the One who is wisdom – the One who spreads out the banquet table – the One who says, *"Come and feed yourself."* It's as if Jesus is taking an encyclopedia and saying, "Open anywhere and enjoy." It's as if He's opening the library and saying, "If you'll fear ME and seek ME, I can make any or all of these books understandable to you." It isn't simple, but God's principles do work. People say, "I can't get something." Jesus says, "I will show you."

I'm not a genius, but I can testify to what God has done for me. I also know that you can accomplish more than you would ever think. It took me years to grasp these principles, and the potential for learning is much greater today. If only we would approach it in a Biblical fashion.

GOD'S LAWS OF LEARNING

THIS PAGE IS FOR YOUR PERSONAL NOTES

CHAPTER 5

FIVE RULES FOR LEARNING

1. **LEARN TO HEAR OR LISTEN**

    "A wise man will hear, and will increase learning;"

    Proverbs 1:5a

    This verse says that "hearing" is directly related to "learning" including how fast and how much a person learns. I'm not talking about being deaf, but rather the process of hearing. A lot of people are exposed to information but never hear it. It went in one ear and out the other. When you turn the teacher off, you also turn the learning off. Not only will the learning not increase, it could grind to an absolute halt. It's wasted time. It's a chosen learning disability.

    Other Scriptures on this subject include...

    "Hear me now therefore, O ye children, and depart not from the words of my mouth."

    Proverbs 5:7

    The Bible is clear – we need to listen. Don't depart from what you hear.

    "A wise son heareth his father's instructions: but a scorner heareth not rebuke."

    Proverbs 13:1

    Some people know how to tune in, while others tune out. A scornful person refuses to hear and learn.

> "...but he that heareth reproof getteth understanding."
>
> **Proverbs 15:32b**

Those people who choose to hear – and receive what they hear – will get some understanding. They will become wise and able to guide their heart in the right direction **(Proverbs 4:10, 19:20, and 23:19:** *Hear, O my son, and receive my sayings; and the years of thy life shall be many.* **Proverbs 4:10,** *Hear counsel, and receive instruction, that thou mayest be wise in thy latter end.* **Proverbs 19:20,** *Hear thou, my son, and be wise, and guide thine heart in the way.* **Proverbs 23:19).**

The Bible is very clear – we're to hear and refuse it not **(Proverbs 8:33)**. These things are directly related to how and what we hear.

When you hear it, don't reject it. Accept and lay hold of it.

If we could just learn to "listen and hear" a lot more of God's Word would stick with us. We must tune in instead of thinking we can gain knowledge by osmosis (absorption through the skin). Some students just sit through the class and then wonder why they didn't get it. But, again, they weren't tuned in to what was being said and it cost them dearly.

Tune in – listen and hear.

2. PAY ATTENTION

> "Hear, ye children, the instruction of a father, and attend to know understanding."
>
> **Proverbs 4:1**

This verse comes mighty close to the matter of hearing. *"Attend to know understanding."* It's one thing to attend school. It's another to pay attention to what the teacher is saying. It's a

CHAPTER 5: FIVE RULES FOR LEARNING

matter of focusing upon what's being said – not thinking about the gym class that's coming up, lunchtime, what to do when school lets out, etc., etc. In other words, "pay attention" to learn and understand. We're not paying attention just to survive the course or satisfy the teacher. We're paying attention to get understanding – to know what's being taught – to know what it means. It won't hurt to ask the teacher what something means or how it applies. What does it involve? The fact that a student would ask the teacher to explain something so he could better understand and not just pass a test is like saying, "Sic 'em, boy" to a dog. Good teachers appreciate that kind of student, the kind who wants to understand what a piece of English literature really has to do with life, or what algebra has to do with living and how it applies.

Pay attention – attend to know.

> *"My son, attend to my words; incline thine ear unto my sayings."*
>
> **Proverbs 4:20**

Don't just go after thoughts. Attend to the very words being spoken. Like it says in the verse, learn to *"incline thine ear."* Turn your ear in the teacher's direction. Strive to hear everything. Don't miss a word – get it all – attend to it carefully.

> *"My son, attend unto my wisdom, and bow thine ear to my understanding."*
>
> **Proverbs 5:1**

If you really want to learn, you'll have a sense of humility, coupled with a desire to honor the teacher. We need to learn to pay attention – with the right attitude – with humility and respect.

3. SEEK AFTER KNOWLEDGE

> *"I love them that love me; and those that seek me early shall find me."*
>
> **Proverbs 8:17**

There must be a sincere desire to learn. During my years of teaching, I came across students who didn't want to learn. They had no interest. My job was to help them overcome that barrier while imparting a hunger or desire for learning. Then, there were those students who really wanted to learn, but couldn't. My job was to give them the confidence they needed to learn and succeed.

The book of Proverbs says, *"...those that seek me early shall find me."* It has to do with *"sound wisdom, understanding, counsel, and strength."*

Proverbs 8:14

Those that say, "I'm hungry for knowledge – I want it – I'm going to search for it – I'm going to dig for it – I'm going to grasp it" – will eventually find it. This is true, whether early in life when one's mind is most pliable and learning is easiest, or later when it's much harder but still possible. Although, it's never too late to learn, there's a distinct advantage to grasping these principles early in life, and early in the day.

> *"The heart of him that hath understanding seeketh knowledge: but the mouth of fools feedeth on foolishness."*
>
> **Proverbs 15:14**

Some people want to constantly jabber foolishness. They have no desire to learn. The Bible says they have the *"mouth of*

CHAPTER 5: FIVE RULES FOR LEARNING

fools." You can divide students that way in churches, schools and the community. God draws a distinction.

> *"Wherefore is there a price in the hand of a fool to get wisdom, seeing he hath no heart to it?"*
>
> **Proverbs 17:16**

When we seek to learn, we need to put our whole heart into it.

> *"Through desire a man, having separated himself, seeketh and intermeddleth with all wisdom. A fool hath no delight in understanding, but that his heart may discover itself."*
>
> **Proverbs 18:1, 2**

In other words, a fool only wants to do what happens to be in his heart. That's the only thing he's interested in. He has no delight in understanding. On the other hand, a wise man is going to seek it out. After all, that's how a person learns. Some people glance over the manual, walk in, and get 100 percent on their driver's test while others have great difficulty. They study long and hard to finally squeeze through. Eventually, they get it. We too can get it; it's a matter of what we desire, and whether we'll stick with it. Do we really desire to learn? Do we hear? Do we seek? Do we have the desire to grasp? If so, are we willing to separate ourselves from other things? We must return to our value system.

Then there is the matter of "intermeddling" by mixing knowledge and wisdom. Saturating – having it around – being exposed to it – and looking at it from all different directions. Yet, some run from the chance to learn instead of jumping right in the middle of it.

Evangelist Billy Kelly loved gravy and biscuits. He once joked he couldn't think of any better way to die, than going down a slide with two big biscuits in each hand, landing in a bowl of gravy, and then drowning while trying to eat it all. This may sound humorous but how many people would truly say, "Just give me the opportunity to see how much I can cram into my mind." What's our heart's desire? We can be as spiritual and knowledgeable as we want. The Bible says, *"...get wisdom, get understanding"* **(Proverbs 4:5, 7).** Get it! – Seek it!

4. **APPLY YOURSELF**

"Bow down thine ear, and hear the words of the wise, and apply thine heart unto my knowledge."

Proverbs 22:17

Apply yourself. A teacher gets up the first day of class and says, "If you're going to make it in this class, you'll have to apply yourself." Or, "Those that apply themselves will likely get A's and B's. Those that don't care may just squeeze by with a D." What is he saying? Applying oneself will make all the difference.

The Word of God is true. These are the same old-fashioned rules of education. Some are still being followed while others are being ignored. Again, the idea of "bowing the ear" is a matter of submission to both knowledge and the teacher.

"Apply thine heart unto instruction, and thine ears to the words of knowledge."

Proverbs 23:12

In **Proverbs 2:2,** it says, *"Apply your heart to understanding."* Apply both your heart and ears. Get your heart involved. Verse 3 says, *"Cry after knowledge."* Real application borders on desperation – crying out to obtain knowledge.

An athlete will never achieve with only mediocre effort.

CHAPTER 5: FIVE RULES FOR LEARNING

Students will never amount to anything if they don't apply themselves. And Christians will never amount to anything if they don't know how to apply themselves.

It's a very simple rule! Apply yourself.

5. **GET IT AND KEEP IT**

> *"Get wisdom, get understanding: forget it not; neither decline from the words of my mouth."*
>
> **Proverbs 4:5**

Get it! – keep it! – don't forget it. From time to time, in our own quietness, we need to stop and think over what we've learned. Hebrews says to be careful about those things you've learned *"lest at any time you let them slip."* Just imagine going through college only to remember 10 percent of what you learned. Get it! – keep it! If you forget, you'll only have to go back and re-learn it. God puts an emphasis on this.

> *"Take fast hold of instruction; let her not go; keep her; for she is thy life."*
>
> **Proverbs 4:13**

> *"He taught me also, and said unto me, Let thine heart retain my words: keep my commandments, and live."*
>
> **Proverbs 4:4**

The concept is retention. Verse 21 of the same chapter says, *"Let them not depart from thine eyes; keep them in the midst of thine heart."*

Get it – keep it – and retain it. Don't forget it.

In **Proverbs 10:14**, the Bible talks about *"laying up knowledge."* This is the same principle as laying up money, treasures, or investments.

I never envisioned the need to know the difference in the relative strengths or the kind of wood fibers in trees, as well as some trigonometry, and the use of a surveyor's instrument, until it came time to choose the lumber and plan the foundation for a new church building. With God's help, we were able to plan and properly layout the foundation while saving money in the process.

Proverbs 6:21 says, *"Bind them continually upon thine heart, and tie them about thy neck."*

Proverbs 7:3 says, *"Bind them upon thy fingers, write them upon the table of thine heart."*

Proverbs 7:1 says, *"Keep my words, and lay up my commandments with thee."*

Get it! – Keep it! – And lay it up.

CHAPTER 6

SIX METHODS OF INSTRUCTION

1. **TEACHING BY PROVERBS**

    "The proverbs of Solomon the son of David, king of Israel; To know wisdom and instruction; to perceive the words of understanding; To receive the instruction of wisdom, justice, and judgment and equity; To give subtility to the simple, to the young man knowledge and discretion."

    Proverbs 1:1-4

    The book of Proverbs was given so that people could get *"knowledge and discretion."* It's another method of teaching. Jesus used parables, illustrations, sayings, and proverbs.

    Today, the use of proverbs, not just Biblical ones, as a method of teaching, has nearly vanished from our public and Christian schools. The reading of Aesop's fables used to be part of one's education. They were considered expanded proverbs. As far as I know, in the U.S., three groups still use proverbs in their teaching, and it's restricted among themselves and in their homes. They are the black people of America, the Indians of America, and the people of the hill culture of the Appalachian Mountains. They're capable of giving a proverb, and of being understood, while making points that the rest of the nation can't even grasp. It's something they keep within themselves. An example would be, "There's more than one way to skin a cat." They use and create dozens and dozens of proverbs to make a point. We need to get back to that. God says it's one way to give "knowledge and discretion."

We should obey what Jesus said in Matthew chapter 7 and verse 6, *"Give not that which is holy unto the dogs, neither cast ye your pearls before swine."* He used parables so that some would understand and others would not. Let me add that there is a difference between clichés and proverbs.

Before we begin to criticize young people for not having discretion, we might ask ourselves, "Is it our fault? Have we applied this method to our teaching?" Proverbs will increase our perception and thus our discretion.

2. **REPROVING**

"Smite a scorner, and the simple will beware; and reprove one that hath understanding, and he will understand knowledge."

Proverbs 19:25

The scorner won't learn, but the simple might. How is *"one that hath understanding"* going to understand knowledge? We can help by reproving or telling them what's wrong. You'll find this same principle in chapter 15 and verse 32. Part of good teaching ought to be reproving.

3. **PROPER USE OF THE ROD AND REPROOF**

"The rod and reproof give wisdom:"

Proverbs 29:15a

Do you realize that you can give wisdom to someone by the proper use of the rod? Do you consider spanking as a teaching process, or just a chance to ventilate your anger? When spanking disappeared from our schools, so did the quality of education. This followed on the heels of removing the very mention of God. When the *"fear of the LORD"* went out so did the matter of being able to get knowledge. We broke God's rules. We threw away the starting point. We eliminated that teaching method. It might not be popular, but it's what God says. Proper use of *"the rod and reproof give wisdom."*

4. TEACH PEOPLE TO FEAR GOD

"The fear of the LORD is the beginning of knowledge; but fools despise wisdom and instruction."

Proverbs 1:7

The *"fear of the LORD"* is another method of teaching. When students learn to fear God, great progress can be made.

- Mathematics has a beautiful balance to its structure and organization. When you teach it right, you can tell students about the One who made math. It becomes, not just a jumble of numbers to struggle with, but fits together as a glorious whole.
- History is the story of God at work.
- Sociology is God working with people.
- Psychology is God working on their minds.
- Science is God's laws in nature.
- Languages were created by God at the tower of Babel.

There are all kinds of interesting things to study. Begin with the *"fear of the LORD."*

5. HEARING WHAT'S SPOKEN

"My son, if thou wilt receive my words, and hide my commandments with thee."

Proverbs 2:1

There's the matter of words being spoken as an effective method of teaching. We can learn a lot by just taking the time to listen to what other people are saying. Properly tuning in can increase one's ability to learn.

6. INSTRUCTION BEING GIVEN

"Hear, ye children, the instruction of a father, and attend to know understanding."

Proverbs 4:1

Typically, the instruction being given could be in the form of preaching or regular teaching. It's the laying down of a principle, then illustrating, teaching, and properly instructing people. It's another way of teaching people and it's mentioned frequently in the book of **Proverbs: 4:13, 8:33, 9:9, 13:1, 19:20, 27, 21:11, 23:23.**

Remember: God has His own rules for learning and His own methods for teaching. If we would just get back to these basic principles, we would know a whole lot more, and so would our students.

CHAPTER 7

DANGERS OF OPPOSING LEARNING

This section addresses the results of opposing or despising learning.

> "The fear of the LORD is the beginning of knowledge; but fools despise wisdom and instruction."
>
> **Proverbs 1:7**

There's a great difference between temporarily learning material to pass a test, versus mastering and permanently storing away what's been learned.

Many people despise wisdom and instruction. Unfortunately, they don't think learning is important. They mock, under-value, and put it down. I've heard students say, "That's stupid. I don't want to learn it." God calls that person a fool. And the mark of a fool is clear; he's going to despise wisdom and knowledge. That's very sobering, but it's what the Bible says.

> "How long, ye simple ones, will ye love simplicity? and the scorners delight in their scorning, and fools hate knowledge?"
>
> **Proverbs 1:22**

Fools not only despise learning – they hate it! Even more frightening are those parents that encourage their children to despise knowledge. I say this very cautiously, although the Word of God is clear. Those parents are programming their sons and daughters to be fools. Instead of encouraging them to learn, they let them think that getting a job is sufficient. It's happening all across America while other nations have students who study, work hard, and place a high value on education. Those that see the need for learning will continue to make progress.

Remember: the Bible says, *"The fool hath said in his heart. There is no God."* Eventually, the person who despises learning won't be interested in almighty God.

Keep on learning – don't despise it.

> *"Then shall they call upon me, but I will not answer; they shall seek me early, but they shall not find me: For that they hated knowledge, and did not choose the fear of the LORD:"*
>
> **Proverbs 1:28, 29**

A person's attitude towards learning will have an effect on getting their prayers answered. God said they'll call upon Him, but He won't answer. This is because *"...they hated knowledge, and didn't choose the fear of the LORD."* This is also a very strong and sobering passage.

If a person will not choose to fear the Lord – if they hate knowledge – it could adversely impact them spiritually. God will not be there in the day of their calamity.

Fear the Lord. Keep on learning. Don't resist it!

> *"And say, How have I hated instruction, and my heart despised reproof: And have not obeyed the voice of my teachers, nor inclined mine ear to them that instructed me!"*
>
> **Proverbs 5:12, 13**

This passage is about disobedient students who weren't

CHAPTER 7: DANGERS OF OPPOSING LEARNING

interested in doing what the teacher said. These students refused to obey and tuned the teacher out. They *"hated instruction and despised reproof."*

Verse 3 describes their nature and warns about the *"lips of a strange woman"* that leads to adultery.

Verse 4 says their end is going to be *"bitter as wormwood, sharp as a twoedged sword."*

Verse 8 warns if they don't get far away from the door of her house, they're in trouble.

Verse 9 refers to giving up their honor and years to the cruel.

Verse 10 says strangers will get their wealth and others will benefit from their labors.

In verse 11 the Bible reads, *"...And thou mourn at the last, when thy flesh and thy body are consumed..."*

These people hated instruction and despised reproof. They refused to obey the voice of their teachers. They were unwilling to incline their ear to their instructors.

In verse 14 we read, *"I was almost in all evil in the midst of the congregation and assembly."*

These people get into churches. They fall into all types of sin. A person's attitude towards learning will show-up in his morals, finances, health, and a myriad of other areas. This is what the Bible teaches.

> *"Whoso loveth instruction loveth knowledge; but he that hateth reproof is brutish."*
>
> **Proverbs 12:1**

Brutish people hate to be reproved – brought to right – and told what is correct and proper. They are by nature what the Bible calls, 'brutish'. What is brutish? It means the person acts like a brute – or bully – physically, emotionally or socially. They 'buck' their way through life. It's another mark of those who refuse to learn.

> *"A fool hath no delight in understanding, but that his heart may discover itself."*
>
> **Proverbs 18:2**

The fool has no interest in learning. He may be interested in surviving the course, but not in understanding. He skims through the material with the intent of squeezing by. A wise person delights, but a *"fool has no delight in understanding."* Unlike the wise person, the fool delights in themselves – in foolishness – in dreams – and in a lack of reality.

CHAPTER 8

THREE THINGS THAT HINDER LEARNING

This section addresses the things that according to the Word of God will hinder people from learning.

1. FOOLISHNESS

> *"A foolish woman is clamorous: she is simple, and knoweth nothing."*
>
> **Proverbs 9:13**

Foolishness is one of the greatest hindrances to learning. God says in verse 6, to *"forsake the foolish and live."* Resist foolishness – it will only hinder you.

> *"The heart of him that hath understanding seeketh knowledge: but the mouth of fools feedeth on foolishness."*
>
> **Proverbs 15:14**

This verse refers to the *"mouth of fools"* – they feed on foolishness – one joke after another – one bit of foolishness after another. A little humor makes a point and lightens the load, but constant foolishness hinders and handicaps learning.

> *"Wisdom is before him that hath understanding; but the eyes of a fool are in the ends of the earth."*
>
> **Proverbs 17:24**

A fool's eyes are looking at the ends of the earth. They are wandering around – daydreaming –looking out the window. Some students could open a book upside down and never notice. Instead of paying attention their mind is on something else. They are not able to focus when they ought to be learning. Those are the eyes of a fool. The mouth feeds on foolishness and the eyes never really get down to studying and learning.

> *"A fool hath no delight in understanding, but that his heart may discover itself."*
>
> **Proverbs 18:2**

The fool is bent on what he wants to do – whatever is his heart's desire. If he wants to dawdle on the paper, then he dawdles on the paper.

> *"Foolishness is bound in the heart of a child; but the rod of correction shall drive it from him."*
>
> **Proverbs 22:15**

What in the world can parents do with a child who is foolish, clamorous, and not interested in learning? The Bible says, "The rod of correction shall drive it far from her." It's both natural and normal for this learning disability or hindrance to occur in the heart of a child. Some have it more deeply rooted than others. Some are more stubborn, but every child has it. Just as *"the rod and reproof give wisdom,"* so does the rod of correction, when properly applied, remove foolishness from the heart of a child. This message is strong, but it's also the Word of God.

2. WICKEDNESS

> *"A wicked doer giveth heed to false lips; and a liar giveth ear to a naughty tongue."*
>
> **Proverbs 17:4**

CHAPTER 8: THREE THINGS THAT HINDER LEARNING

Some people are constantly being deceived because they have a nature that's bent that way. Wickedness is a hindrance to learning. A wicked person will follow people who say and teach wrongly. A liar is going to give ear to a naughty tongue.

Sin hampers learning. That's why public schools and universities once had moral and strict standards regarding right and wrong. They were not interested in making students into Christians, but they wanted them to learn more readily.

I have known brilliant, well-grounded students, who didn't graduate from high school because they couldn't handle the courses. They had adopted a pattern of living in sin. I've also seen that when poor students became saved God resurrected their learning power. Their hindrance to learning was removed.

Proverbs 28:5a reads, *"Evil men understand not judgment."* Sin is a hindrance to learning. Wickedness deprives people of a clear understanding of judgment.

3. LISTENING TO WRONG TEACHING

> *"Cease, my son, to hear the instruction that causeth to err from the words of knowledge."*
>
> **Proverbs 19:27**

One of the hindrances to learning is listening to the wrong kind of teaching. Some teaching will cause people to shipwreck: spiritually, financially, and/or intellectually. Be cautious, look at what the teaching is producing. Quit listening to every teacher who comes along. If an economics teacher can't balance his checkbook, do you really want to take his bookkeeping course? Such a teacher might give every student an A, but he'll also cause them to err.

GOD'S LAWS OF LEARNING

Be careful. Seek qualified teachers.

CHAPTER 9

THREE PROBLEMS OF IGNORANCE

The following problems are in addition to being handicapped for life and labeled a "fool" by God.

1. DESTRUCTION

> "Wise men lay up knowledge: but the mouth of the foolish is near destruction."
>
> **Proverbs 10:14**

Destruction is ahead for those people who won't learn. It could be national destruction when a country refuses to learn. It could be statewide, city-wide, or regional destruction when an area refuses to learn or gives up trying. Maybe it's a personal destruction or the loss of liberty and freedoms. Add to that economic destruction – social destruction – destruction by war – and spiritual destruction. These usually occur because people won't learn. For those that choose not to learn, destruction is just up the road. Even though the Bible has warned them, when the rug comes out from under them, it often catches them by surprise.

2. DEATH

> "The lips of the righteous feed many: but fools die for want of wisdom."
>
> **Proverbs 10:21**

How many people took the wrong medicine and died because they didn't learn what they needed to know? Maybe the person's dreams or hopes for the future died – or their marriage crumbled – because of a lack of wisdom. These people chose not to learn – they lacked wisdom – and it cost them greatly.

I want you to know, this information has been written in God's record for three thousand years. God has preserved its accuracy down through the centuries. It has always been and always will be so. God put it in the Bible for our own benefit.

We ought to believe it – and act on it.

3. FINANCES

> *"Wherefore is there a price in the hand of a fool to get wisdom, seeing he hath no heart to it?"*
>
> **Proverbs 17:16**

Money won't improve the education of a fool. It takes a changed heart. I don't understand Christian parents who choose not to learn themselves, and don't want their children to learn either. God gave them a new heart, yet they don't want to learn from Him. The Word of God speaks very clearly about the need to keep on learning.

If students refuse to learn – if they won't incline the ear to instruction – if they disobey teachers, despise knowledge, and hate school – then the money spent is wasted. They might get grades on a piece of paper, a diploma at the end, but they'll be as ill-prepared as if they'd dropped out.

God has laws for learning. If we would only get back to the Bible, we would see what He could do for those that obey and honor His Word. *"Those that will seek the LORD can know all things."*

INDEX OF WORDS AND PHRASES

abilities, 24, 31, 34
academic, 26
altar of education, 37
apply themselves, 44, 45
attitude, 31, 34, 35, 41, 52, 53
Babylonians, 16
beginning of knowledge, 22, 23, 24, 25, 32, 35, 49, 51
Bible, 2, 5, 11, 13, 14, 15, 22, 23, 26, 30, 33, 39, 40, 42, 44, 45, 51, 52, 53, 56, 59, 60, 65
Billy Kelly, 44
Birth, 13
bitter, 53
black, 47
born smart, 13
brutish, 35, 53
Cain, 17
Chaldeans, 16
child, 14, 21, 24, 56
Daniel, 16, 26
despise, 22, 51, 52, 60
destruction, 36, 59
disciplined, 34
economic destruction, 59
education collapses, 21
English, 26, 32, 41
evil, 31, 32, 53

eyes, 16, 31, 33, 45, 55
Finances, 60
folly, 35, 36
fool, 22, 35, 36, 43, 51, 52, 54, 55, 56, 59, 60
fools despise wisdom and instruction, 49, 51
from a child, 14
genius, 24, 37
getting smart, 13
grammar, 32
Greek, 15, 32
Harvard University, 32
Harvey, 3
hear, 13, 22, 39, 40, 41, 43, 44, 57
Hebrew, 16, 32
heredity, 13
Herman, 3
history, 22, 26
humble, 33
Indians, 47
IQ, 11, 24
Jacob, 17, 26
Jesus, 14, 15, 36, 37, 47, 48
Joseph, 16, 26
KJV, 5
Laban, 17
languages, 22, 25, 26, 32
laws of learning, 13, 17

61

learn in the wrong place, 21
listen, 39, 40, 50
man of knowledge, 20
Mathematics, 49
merchandise, 29
mock, 35, 51
money, 23, 30, 45, 46, 60
pearls before swine, 48
Pharaoh, 16
picture language, 33
Plato, 36
politeness of speech, 34
political training, 17
possibilities, 19
pride, 33
priorities, 30
promises, 19
proverbs, 47, 48
prudent, 33, 34, 35
Psychology, 49
Pythagorean factor, 36
reading, 5, 11, 14, 15, 47
Reno, 1, 2, 3, 5, 11
reproof, 2, 35, 40, 48, 49, 52, 53, 56
retention, 45
rod, 48, 56
rod of correction, 56
rubies, 29, 30
rules, 13, 44, 49, 50
Science, 49
scorner, 21, 39, 48
Scriptures, 14, 15, 17, 39
seek me early, 34, 35, 42, 52

Seminary, 15
shipwreck, 57
sights, 14
silver, 16, 23, 29, 30
simple ones, 51
sin, 32, 37, 53, 57
sincere desire to learn, 42
Sociology, 49
Socrates, 36
Solomon, 47
sounds, 14
spiritual destruction, 59
storage room, 13
study, 5, 15, 20, 22, 43, 49, 52
sweetness of the lips, 33, 34
television, 35
think, 11, 13, 14, 26, 31, 34, 37, 44, 45, 51
time, 17, 19, 21, 26, 32, 39, 45, 46, 50, 65
Timothy, 7, 14, 26
trigonometry, 46
unique ability, 20
Vivian, 3
wealth, 29, 30, 53
wisdom, 15, 16, 19, 20, 21, 22, 23, 24, 25, 29, 30, 33, 34, 36, 37, 41, 42, 43, 44, 45, 47, 48, 51, 56, 59, 60
wise man, 13, 20, 39, 43
work, 17, 21, 22, 24, 36, 37, 49, 52, 65
wormwood, 53

CHAPTER 8: THREE THINGS THAT HINDER LEARNING

wrong foundation, 21
yard sale, 20

THIS PAGE IS FOR YOUR PERSONAL NOTES

GOD'S LAWS OF LEARNING

THIS PAGE IS FOR YOUR PERSONAL NOTES

ABOUT THE AUTHOR

J. PAUL RENO has been a pastor in Ohio and Maryland since 1968. During this time he has also been involved in church planting, training men for the ministry and speaking on mission fields in Europe, the Middle East, Africa, South America and Mexico. The church he presently pastors has just passed sending over three million dollars to missions. He continues to speak at various Bible conferences, camp meetings and local churches. He presently serves on the Board of Directors for the Conversion Center, which is headquartered in Hagerstown, Maryland. He has also written *To Fight or Not to Fight*, as well as over fifty pamphlets and booklets on salvation, the Christian life, Bible doctrine and the King James Version. His wife, Carolyn authored *Almost But Lost*, available as a free ebook download at

http://www.theoldpathspublications.com/Pages/Free.htm.

Paul is the father of five children, all of whom are active in the Lord's work with three serving presently as missionaries in Brazil.

THIS PAGE IS FOR YOUR PERSONAL NOTES

THIS PAGE IS FOR YOUR PERSONAL NOTES

1

www.ingramcontent.com/pod-product-compliance
Lightning Source LLC
Chambersburg PA
CBHW060427050426
42449CB00009B/2169